IMAGES OF
SPORT

HEART OF MIDLOTHIAN
FOOTBALL CLUB

STADIA

IMAGES OF
SPORT

HEART OF MIDLOTHIAN
FOOTBALL CLUB

HEART OF MIDLOTHIAN FOOTBALL CLUB

First published 1998
Reprinted 2003
STADIA edition 2006

STADIA is an imprint of
Tempus Publishing Limited
The Mill, Brimscombe Port,
Stroud, Gloucestershire, GL5 2QG
www.tempus-publishing.com

British Library Cataloguing in Publication Data.
A catalogue record for this book is available from the British Library.

ISBN 0 7524 1560 3

Typesetting and origination by Tempus Publishing Limited.
Printed in Great Britain.

Contents

Introduction		7
Acknowledgements		8
1.	The Pioneer Years	9
2.	The First Golden Era	17
3.	Great Years in the Scottish Cup	25
4.	The Years of Conflict	33
5.	War Again and Beyond	67
6.	The Fabulous Fifties	79
7.	Hearts in the Sixties and Seventies	93
8.	The Eighties	107
9.	The Nineties	121

Alan Anderson scores against Celtic in March 1966. This epic cup-tie ended in a 3-3 draw.

Introduction

This insight into the rich history of Heart of Midlothian FC was compiled and written by avid collectors of club memorabilia; David Speed, Bill Smith, Graham Blackwood and John Kerr.

These life-long Hearts supporters are fascinated by the story of the club from its humble roots in the old town of Edinburgh and have on record every known match result, together with detailed information about players and events over the last 125 years, compiled from external research and the books preserved by the club.

David, Bill, Graham and John want to promote the fame of Hearts as widely as possible and their historical and statistical work is regularly included in official club publications. This book will be valued by all those supporters who share this love of the traditions and achievements of this wonderful football club.

At last! The Scottish Cup arrives back at Tynecastle, May 1998.

Acknowledgements

Thanks are due to the following individuals and organisations for their help with this publication:

Irene McPhee of Heart of Midlothian FC, Andrew Hoggan, the *Edinburgh Evening News*, *The Scotsman*, the *Scottish Daily Express*, the *Scottish Daily Mail*, and the *Daily Record*.

One

The Pioneer Years

THE HEART OF MIDLOTHIAN.

The Tolbooth of Edinburgh, which was demolished in 1817, was known locally as the 'Heart of Midlothian.' Sir Walter Scott immortalized the name in his writings and many institutions were named after this old jail – including the Heart of Midlothian dancing hall in Washing Green Court, off the South Bank Canongate. A group of young lads who frequented the dancing club formed a football team, playing under local rules. However, after Queen's Park and Clydesdale played an exhibition match in the city in December 1873, the dancers adopted association rules and the reformed club was called Heart of Midlothian after their other favourite pastime. This was during the early months of 1874, when matches were played on the East Meadows and the club's headquarters were established at Mother Anderson's Tavern on West Cross Causeway.

Hearts playing squad in 1875, wearing the club's original strip of all-white with a maroon heart on the breast. The club was strong enough to join the Scottish Football Association and the Edinburgh Football Association. In the 1875/76 season, the club took part in the Scottish Cup and the Edinburgh FA Cup (later the East of Scotland Shield) for the first time.

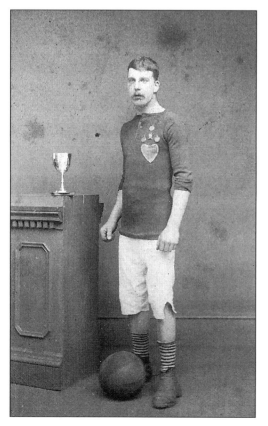

A young Tom Purdie, the first captain of Hearts and one of the toughest defenders of his day. Tom led the players through the streets from Anderson's Tavern to the pitches next to Boroughloch Brewery, until a stripping box was erected in 1876 at the Meadow's Schoolhouse.

In September 1876, due to a shortage of members, Hearts informed the Edinburgh FA that it had disbanded. The club also withdrew from the Scottish Cup. However, the bulk of the playing staff joined St Andrew's FC and, by the end of the year, Hearts re-appeared, having absorbed Saints members and players. The strip was now changed to red, white and blue hoops.

Edinburgh FA Cup winners in 1878, the first trophy won by the club. Hibs were defeated in the fourth replay of the final by a Hearts team which had now dyed its red, white and blue shirts to maroon. The successful players were, from left to right, back row: G. Barbour, J. Whitson, J. Reid, J. Sweenie, J. Alexander. Middle row: H. Wyllie, R. Winton, J. Burns, G. Mitchell. Front row (seated): T. Purdie, A. Lees.

Hearts with the President's Cup in May 1879. The club was still playing its home matches on the East Meadows, but important fixtures were held at the Edinburgh FA ground at Powburn. The club's headquarters were now at McKenzie's sports shop in Chapel Street.

Nick Ross, a star of his era, both for Hearts and Preston North End, who were the leading club in England at this time. He saw Hearts become strong enough to secure a private ground at Powderhall in 1879 and notch up a record victory of 21-0 versus Anchor FC in the EFA Cup tie of October 1880.

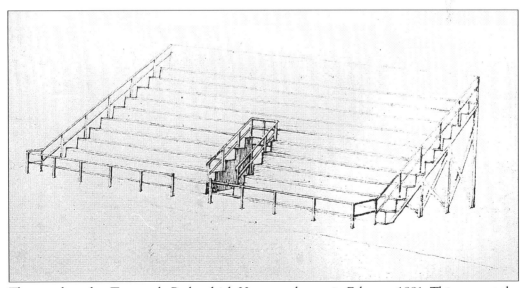

The grandstand at Tynecastle Park, which Hearts took over in February 1881. This was not the present ground but stood at the site of what is now Wardlaw Street and Wardlaw Place.

Winners of the initial competition for the Rosebery Charity Cup in the 1882/83 season. Hearts were strong locally, but that year suffered an 8-1 defeat in the Scottish Cup at the hands of Vale of Leven. This remained the club's record defeat for nearly 100 years.

Johnny Gair, one of many Hearts stars who were lured into the professional game in England. This allowed Hibs to dominate the scene and forced Hearts to make illegal payments to players, resulting in an SFA suspension in October 1884. After a new committee was elected, Hearts were re-admitted to the SFA.

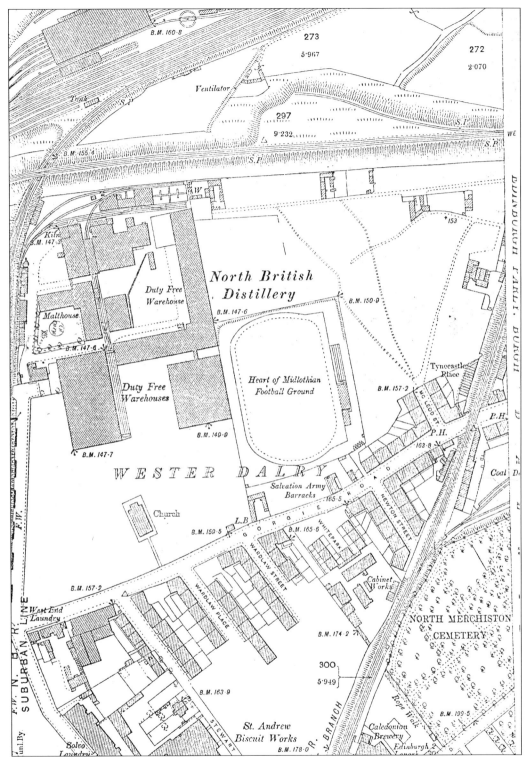

In April 1886, Hearts opened the present Tynecastle Park with a 4-1 win over Bolton Wanderers. The club also met English opposition when it entered the FA Cup in 1886/87, but suffered a heavy 7-1 reverse in Lancashire against Darwen FC.

With Hibs in decline following the formation of Celtic, Hearts began a period of unequivocal domination in local football in the late 1880s. In this 1889/90 team group, the Rosebery Charity Cup and the Edinburgh FA Shield are displayed. Tom Jenkinson, sitting on the left, was the first Hearts man to be selected for Scotland when he was called up in February 1887 for the game versus Ireland.

Hearts were founder members of the Scottish League in the 1890/91 season and finished sixth in the inaugural competition. However, the players did achieve national fame at long last when Dumbarton were beaten 1-0 in the Scottish Cup Final of February 1891. The winning players were, from left to right, middle row: Adams, Fairbairn, Russell, Begbie, Hill, Goodfellow, McPherson. Front row: Taylor, Mason (the goalscorer), Scott, Baird.

Two

The First Golden Era

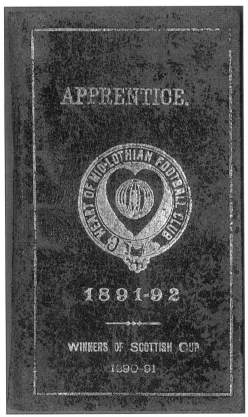

A boy's season ticket from 1891/92, on which the club's first national honour is proudly recorded. The supporters were also proud to see Tynecastle Park host a full international for the first time when Scotland defeated Wales 6-1 on 26 March 1892.

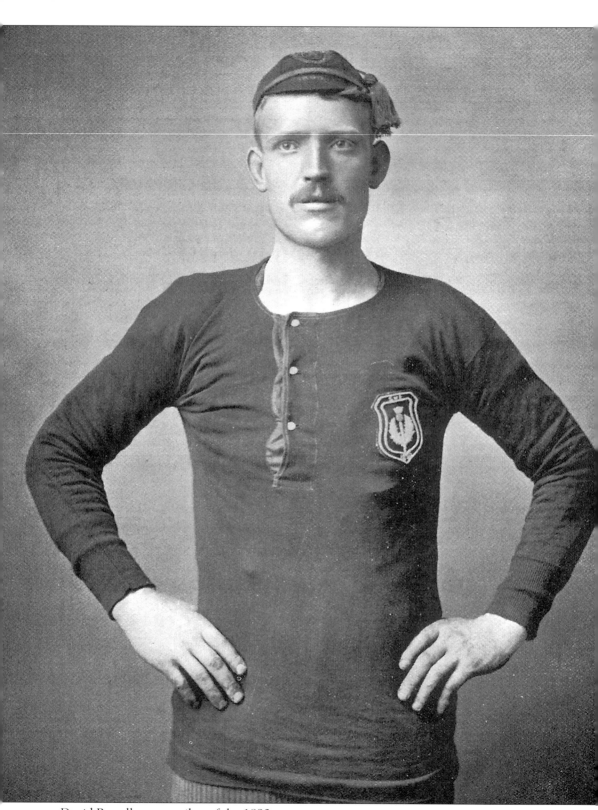

David Russell, a star striker of the 1890s.

Issac Begbie, a great club servant and inspirational captain. He was a Gorgie boy and spent twelve years with the club from 1888. Issac's resolute ball-winning earned him four Scotland caps and he led Hearts to two League Championships and two Scottish Cup Final victories. He was also one of Hearts' first professional players when the paying of individuals was sanctioned by the SFA in May 1893.

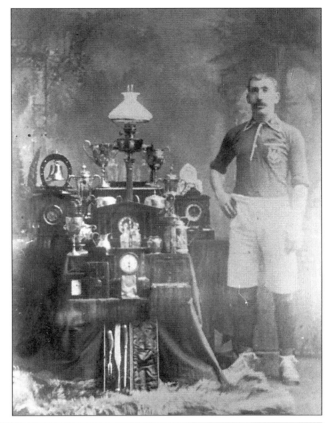

In the season of 1894/95, Hearts won the League Championship for the first time. Here are the players and officials who steered the club to this historic achievement. From left to right, back row: R. Waugh, R. Cheyne, B. Battles, J. Stirling, R. Smith, W. Cox, W. Lorimer, J. Mirk, J. Cairns, W. Amos, G. Hogg, J. Adams. Middle row (seated): R. McLaren, W. Michael, I. Begbie (Captain), A. Hall, G. Scott. Seated on ground: T. Chambers, J. Walker.

George Hogg, one of the stars of Hearts' first championship-winning squad. The 'Tynecastle Warhorse' was signed from Mossend Swifts in 1891 and earned two League Championships and two Scottish Cup winners' medals during his career. He played twice for Scotland.

Action from the 1896 Scottish Cup Final, in which Hearts defeated Hibs 3-1 to lift the trophy for a second time.

Hearts' defence in action during the 1896 Cup Final, which was played before a full-house of 17,000 at Logie Green, Edinburgh (the home of St Bernards FC). This remains the only Scottish Cup Final to be played outside Glasgow.

The 1896 Scottish Cup Final kicks off. Hearts scored after three minutes through a Davie Baird penalty kick and Alex King made the score 2-0 early in the second half. Willie Michael headed a third before Hibs scored a consolation goal.

The Scottish Cup winners. From left to right, standing (players only): Bob McCartney, Jock Fairbairn, James Mirk. Middle row (seated): Bob McLaren, Willie Michael, Johnny Walker, George Hogg, Issac Begbie, David Russell. Seated on ground: Davie Baird, Alex King.

In the 1896/97 season, Hearts won the League Championship for the second time, forcing Hibs into second place during the final weeks of the campaign. The main players are featured here, from left to right, standing: David Baird, Willie Taylor, James Sharp, Johnny Walker, J. Chapman (Trainer), Jock Fairbairn, James Mirk, Harry Marshall. Seated: George Hogg, Bob McCartney, Bob McLaren , Issac Begbie.

David Baird, possibly Hearts' most versatile performer. Born in Edinburgh, this fast and elusive ball player played for the club from 1888 to 1904, appearing on the wing, in midfield and at full-back. He won two winners' medals in the League Championship and three in the Scottish Cup. Davie also played three times for Scotland.

The illustrious Bobby Walker was a local boy who signed for Hearts in April 1896 from Dalry Primrose FC. The teenage playmaker would spread the fame of the club throughout Europe and eventually earned twenty-nine caps for Scotland – still a record for a Hearts man.

Three

Great Years in the Scottish Cup

In 1901, Hearts won the Scottish Cup for the third time. The Tynecastle heroes are pictured here. From left to right, back row: Bob Waugh (Trainer), Davie Baird, Albert Buick, George Hogg, George Philip, Harry Allan. Middle row: George Key, Bobby Walker, Charlie Thomson, Bob Houston. Seated on ground: Bill Porteous, Mark Bell.

Hearts and Tottenham Hotspur played home and away in cup-winners' challenge matches during the 1901/02 season. This was promoted as a 'World Championship' event and Hearts drew the first leg 0-0 in London. The return game at Tynecastle ended in a 3-1 victory for the 'Maroons'.

The Edinburgh Tramways brake which carried the 1901 Cup winners in triumph through the streets of Edinburgh. Celtic were beaten 4-3 in the final with Bobby Walker, Mark Bell (2) and Charlie Thomson scoring the goals. With the game finely balanced at 3-3, it was the 'pacey' Mark Bell who scored a sensational winner for Hearts.

At the turn of the century, fund-raising events became crucial for clubs and the Hearts prize draw was organized by the club's first secretary-manager, Peter Fairley. Income was also generated from bill posting, track rental, publications and refreshment bars.

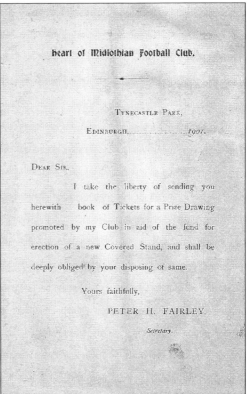

Heart of Midlothian Football Club.

TYNECASTLE PARK,

EDINBURGH, _____ 1901.

DEAR SIR,

I take the liberty of sending you herewith book of Tickets for a Prize Drawing promoted by my Club in aid of the fund for erection of a new Covered Stand, and shall be deeply obliged by your disposing of same.

Yours faithfully,

PETER H. FAIRLEY.

Secretary.

Most of the players who participated in the 1903 Scottish Cup Final are featured in this picture. Unfortunately, Hearts lost 2-0 to Rangers in the third replay of the final, at Celtic Park. The same squad finished as runners-up in the League Championship table of the 1903/04 season.

The Heart of Midlothian Football Club,
Limited.

REPORT BY THE DIRECTORS

TO THE

FIRST ANNUAL GENERAL MEETING OF SHAREHOLDERS, to be held at ST CUTHBERT'S HALL, KING'S STABLES ROAD, EDINBURGH, on FRIDAY, 23rd MARCH 1906, at 7.30 o'clock P.M.

The Directors beg to report that the Revenue for the period from 19th May 1905 to 7th March 1906 amounted to . . £5843 1 9
while the Expenditure amounted to . . . 5500 5 2

Leaving a Profit for the period of . . . £342 16 7
which the Directors recommend should be applied as follows :—
To Reserve Fund £300 0 0
Carried forward to next year 42 16 7
£342 16 7

All the Directors retire at this time. As only the present nine Directors were nominated at the Meeting on 27th ult., they will be re-elected.

Mr. W. D. Stewart, C.A., the Auditor, also retires, and as he was nominated at the Meeting on the 27th ult., will be re-elected.

Shareholders who have paid the full amount due on their Shares will be forwarded their Share Certificates on sending Mr. W. D. Stewart. C.A., 18 Duke Street, their Allotment Letter with Banker's Receipts.

WM. LORIMER,
Chairman.

W. LINDSAY WAUGH,
Secretary.

EDINBURGH, 15th March 1906.

Page one of the first directors' report of The Heart of Midlothian FC Limited. The club actually became a limited company in 1903, but this concern was wound-up in 1905 after financial difficulties.

Despite the club's financial difficulties, Hearts won the Scottish Cup in 1906 by defeating Third Lanark 1-0 in the final with a George Wilson goal. The team group shows nine of the victorious players (D. Philip and G. Couper are missing). From left to right, back row: G. Goodfellow (Assistant Trainer), G. Philip, D. Bain, F. McLaren, H. McNaught, W. Waugh (Manager), J. Chapman (Trainer). Front row: D. Lindsay, R. Walker, A. Menzies, C. Thomson (Captain), J. Dickson, D. Wilson, G. Wilson.

Hearts in 1907. Despite the loss of George Wilson (to Everton), David Wilson (to Everton) and Alex Menzies (to Manchester United), the team battled through to the Scottish Cup Final. However, Celtic proved too strong and Hearts went down 3-0 in the club's sixth cup final.

Hearts masterful centre half, Charlie Thomson , who was signed in 1898 from Prestonpans FC and played in the Scottish Cup-winning teams of 1901 and 1906. He also earned twelve international caps before moving to Sunderland in 1908 together with Tom Allan for a joint fee of £700. This was a major blow to manager James McGhee's restructuring plans.

Tynecastle Park, showing the new stand which was built in 1903 by linking three separate structures.

George Wilson, the scorer of Hearts'
winning goal in the 1906 Scottish
Cup Final against Third Lanark.
The strong and direct international
winger came from Cowdenbeath in
1903 and was transferred to Everton
in May 1906.

G. WILSON, Heart of Mid-lothian.

The squad which finished eleventh
in the League campaign of 1908/09.
Things did not improve the
following season and manager James
McGhee (middle row, second from
right) resigned and was replaced by
John McCartney in January 1910.

TELEPHONE Nº 61321.   TELEPHONE (HOUSE) Nº 62130.

GROUNDS, TYNECASTLE PARK

HEART OF MID-LOTHIAN FOOTBALL CLUB, LIMITED.

Wᴹ Mᶜ CARTNEY, Secy.

(REGISTERED ADDRESS.)

Tynecastle Park, Gorgie Road,

Edinburgh, 11 _____ 19

Hearts badge that was used for most of the pre-Second World War years.

Hearts in action against Rangers in 1910. Frank McLaren is in the darker shirt.

Four

The Years of Conflict

Manager, John McCartney, and his successful reserve team in 1911.

G. Sinclair, Hearts

After finishing as runners-up in the 1905/06 Championship, Hearts had five poor seasons of League football and even finished fourteenth in 1910/11, the club's lowest placing at that time. However, individuals such as George Sinclair still attracted the crowds to Tynecastle. This fine winger was signed from Leith Athletic in 1908 and earned three full international and three League caps during his career. He was one of the courageous Hearts who volunteered for service during the First World War.

ROSEBERY CHARITY CUP TIE

Under the distinguished Patronage of the Lord Provost and Town Council of Edinburgh, and the Provost and Town Council of Leith

HEARTS

KICK-OFF
AT **330** P.M.
To be Played
to a Finish.

VERSUS

Over
£6000
has been allocated
to Charitable Insti-
tutions throughout
the City & District

HIBS

CUP HOLDERS

TYNECASTLE PARK
GORGIE ROAD

On **SATURDAY, 10th MAY 1913**

A common sight around the city before the outbreak of war.

Hearts in 1913. From left to right, back row: A. Lyon (Assistant Trainer), E. Bannister, R. Mercer, P. Dawson, T. Allan, R. Walker, D. Taylor, R. Currie and J. Duckworth (Trainer). Middle row: G. Sinclair, W. Macpherson, F. McLaren, L. Abrams, P. Nellies. Front row, seated on ground: T. Hegarty and G. Whitehead. Most of these men helped Hearts to the Scottish Cup Semi-final in 1911/12 and to fourth place in the League. They also took Hearts to third place in 1912/13 and to a second successive Scottish Cup Semi-final.

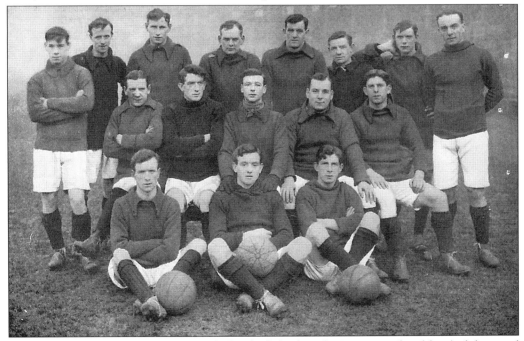

Hearts squad in 1913/14, when the side finished third in the League with a (then) club record of fifty-four points. From left to right, back row: W. Wilson, H. Wattie, P. Dawson, T. Allan, R. Currie, G. Sinclair, P. Crossan, D. Taylor. Middle row: A. Briggs, D. Currie, C. Hallwood, L. Abrams, W. Scott. Front row, seated on ground: R. Malcolm, J. Frew, J. Ness.

Hearts' brilliant striker, Percy Dawson, who was transferred to Blackburn Rovers in February 1914 for the (then) astonishing fee of £2,500. Dawson scored over 100 goals in four seasons at Tynecastle, following his recruitment from North Shields Athletic. His transfer allowed Hearts to proceed with the construction of the present main stand, which cost £12,000.

The Hearts touring party on the club's second overseas tour in 1914. The 'Maroons' recorded a famous 2-1 victory over the Danish international team, thanks to two goals from Willie Wilson (middle row, third from right). This side would almost have certainly won the League Championship in the 1914/15 season, but for one of the most heroic acts in the club's history.

Hearts manager, John McCartney, who created the team that finished as runners-up to Celtic in the 1914/15 League Championship. During the season, the First World War broke out in Europe and, in November 1914, the entire first team, together with 400 shareholders and season ticket holders, volunteered to defend their country, the first football club in Britain to do so. Players were called away and military training sapped their strength. Accordingly, the Championship slipped from Hearts' grasp in the final weeks of the season.

The following pictures are of seven Hearts' heroes. Sergeant Duncan Currie, killed while leading his platoon at the Somme offensive, 1 July 1916.

Sergeant John Allan, killed at Roeux, near Arras, 22 April 1917.

Corporal Thomas Gracie, died at Stobhill War Hospital, Glasgow, 23 October 1915.

Lance-corporal James Boyd, killed at the Somme, 3 August 1916.

Private James Speedie, killed at Loos, 25 September 1915.

Private Ernest Ellis, killed at the Somme, 1 July 1916.

Private Harry Wattie, killed at the Somme, 1 July 1916.

Hearts players at the Front.
1. Gracie 2. Currie 3. Wattie 4. Crossan
5. Frew 6. Sinclair 7. Findlay 8. Ness
9. Briggs 10. Ellis 11. Speedie 12. Wilson
13. Low.

A souvenir postcard featuring the illustrious Bobby Walker. This was issued in connection with the Belgian Relief Fund match at Tynecastle in April 1915, one of many events that the club organised to support the war effort.

Andy Wilson, the former Middlesbrough and Scotland striker, inspired Hearts to the Victory Cup Final in the 1918/19 season. This was the club's best performance during the four years of the war, but the 'Maroons' went down 3-0 to St Mirren in the final at Celtic Park. That year, Wilson became the first Hearts player to score thirty goals in a League campaign and forty over a season.

Bob Mercer, 'the mastermind of modern football', and a stalwart for Hearts between 1908 and 1921. The powerful centre half came from Leith Athletic and would have earned more than two Scottish caps but for his war service, which saw him severely gassed. Bob went to Dunfermline in 1921 and returned to coach Hearts' youngsters. Tragically, due to his war experiences, he collapsed and died on the pitch at Selkirk while leading a young Tynecastle team.

Hearts in 1919. In the back row, second from left, is William McCartney, who took over as Hearts manager in November 1919 at the age of thirty. The former First Division referee replaced his father John McCartney in the Tynecastle 'hotseat'.

SCOTTISH NAT WAR MEMORIAL MATCH TYNECASTLE PARK MAY 22ND 1920
HEARTS OF MIDLOTHIAN v CELTIC

Tynecastle Park in 1920. The main stand was erected in 1914, while the covered enclosure on the distillery side dates from 1911. In September 1919, a (then) record League crowd of 40,700 watched a fixture against Celtic.

George Miller, a smooth and silky inside forward whom Hearts signed from Tranent Juniors in 1915. He was capped in the Victory international against Ireland in 1919 and it was hoped that he would be a key man in the club's post-war rebuilding plans. Unfortunately, George had a well-paid job and could not accept full-time terms. He joined Raith Rovers in 1922, but returned to Tynecastle in 1925 for a fee of £1,000.

Hearts in 1919/20, when the team finished sixteenth in the League. The ageing Tynecastle side recovered the following season, to finish third and reach the Scottish Cup Semi-finals.

STRINGFELLOW, Heart of Midlothian.

Hearts slumped to nineteenth in the twenty-two club Scottish League in 1921/22. To avoid relegation, the 'Maroons' had to win at Aberdeen on the final day of the season and did so, thanks to a goal from Frank Stringfellow (pictured). The 5ft 5in striker, who came from Portsmouth for a £1,100 fee, knocked in the only goal in the second half to cheers from the entire Pittodrie crowd.

BLOCK B

Heart of Midlothian Football Club.

*The Board of Management request the honour
of your presence at the Unveiling of the War
Memorial, which they have erected at Haymarket
to the Memory of their Players and Members
who fell in the Great War.*

*The Unveiling Ceremony will be performed by
The Right Hon. Robert Munro, K. C., M. P.,
on Sunday, 9th April 1922, at 3 p.m.*

*Tynecastle Park,
Edinburgh.*

An invitation to the unveiling of the club's war memorial in April 1922. The Secretary of State for Scotland told the 35,000 onlookers that 'Hearts had shown on the battlefield that courage, resource, skill, endurance, dash and daring that made them famous on the football field'.

The Heart of Midlothian War Memorial, still a famous landmark in the city.

(TOP ROW) CROSSAN, W. WHITE, WILSON. (CENTRE ROW) W. McCARTNEY, DAND, RAMAGE, KING, T. MURPHY.
(SECY. & MANAGER)   (TRAINER)
(FRONT ROW) MURPHY, J. WHITE, GREEN, MacMILLAN, MURRAY.

Hearts in the 1924/25 season. The squad had been dramatically restructured after that relegation scare and defeat in the Scottish Cup by Second Division Bo'ness, in January 1923. The new men in the picture were – Willie White (from Hamilton), John White (Albion Rovers), Tom Green (Clapton Orient), Lachie McMillan (Hamilton) and Willie Murray (Middlesbrough).

The tough and dependable Jock Ramage, who was a stalwart in the Hearts defence during the immediate post-war seasons, when manager Willie McCartney struggled to find that winning combination. Jock was signed in September 1919 from Bonnyrigg Rose and was captain of the team from 1924 to 1926. He received a benefit match against Preston North End in September 1924 and two years later Coventry City paid £1,200 for his transfer.

Hearts defeated Dundee United 6-0 in the Scottish Cup at Tynecastle in February 1926. Jock White scored four goals that day and also in Hearts' next two competitive fixtures (against Alloa and Hamilton). His hat-trick of four goals is unsurpassed in British football. Unfortunately, Hearts lost in the Third Round to Celtic in front of a new Tynecastle record attendance of 51,000.

Hearts against Kilmarnock in 1926. The 'Maroons' finished a creditable third in the League in 1925/26, but fell back to thirteenth the following season.

The illustrious John White, a high-class poacher who was idolised by the Tynecastle fans. The international striker cost £2,700 when he was signed from Albion Rovers in May 1922 and Leeds United paid a near-British record fee of £5,700 when they took him to England in February 1927. This incredible fee allowed the club to complete a massive renovation of the stadium terraces between 1925 and 1929.

Hearts squad at Portsmouth in September 1926, where a benefit match was played against the local club. The game ended in a 1-1 draw.

Hearts team at the start of the 1928/29 season. From left to right, back row: William McCartney (Manager), Andy Herd, Hugh Shaw, Jack Harkness, Bob King, unknown, Bob Bennie. Front row: Jimmy Smith, Barney Battles, Peter Kerr, Lachie McMillan, Willie Murray. For the second successive season, Hearts finished fourth in the League, inspired by goal-grabber Barney Battles and notable signings Peter Kerr (Hibs), Andy Herd (Dunfermline), Hugh Shaw (Rangers), Jack Harkness (Queen's Park) and Bob Bennie (Airdrie).

Hearts players returned from a summer tour of Scandinavia looking fit and healthy, but this was not reflected in the results with the team finishing tenth in 1929/30. The 'Maroons' reached the Scottish Cup Semi-finals, but lost 4-1 to Rangers at Hampden Park before 92,048 spectators.

Hearts magnificent goalscorer, Barney Battles, who was born in Fisherrow, but spent his formative years in the USA, where he played international football while with Boston AL. Barney joined Hearts in July 1928 and, before he retired in 1936, hit a superb total of 218 goals (134 in the League). This included a club record forty-four League goals in 1930-31, when Hearts were fifth in the table.

Tynecastle on 13 February 1932, when an all-time record attendance of 53,396 watched Rangers defeat Hearts 1-0 in the third round of the Scottish Cup. The team fell to eighth place in the League that season.

Hearts in 1932/33. From left to right, back row: William McCartney (Manager), Alex Massie, Andy Anderson, Jack Harkness, Tom O'Neill, John Johnstone, Bob Bennie. Front row: Bob Johnstone, Jock White, Barney Battles, Jimmy Smith, Willie Murray.

Heart of Midlothian Football Club Limited
1932=33

OFFICIAL PROGRAMME

Directors:
WM. C. P. BROWN, Esq., J.P., Chairman.

E. H. FURST, Esq., J.P., Vice-Chairman   GEO. G. L. M'KAY, Esq.
WM. BROWN, Esq.   THOMAS WATERSTON, Esq.
WM. C. SIMPSON, Esq.   DAVID BAIRD, Esq.
JAS. G. ROBERTSON, Esq.

Secretary & Manager: *Telephone:*   *Registered Office:*
WM. M'Cartney.   Edinburgh 61321.   Tynecastle Park, Edinburgh.

No. 4.   **HEARTS v. CELTIC.**   October 1 1932

EDITOR'S NOTES·

The untimely end of our young player, Robert Burns, came as a great shock to all those who knew him, and particularly to the management, players, and training staff at Tynecastle. Robert was a prime favourite, and the death of this promising footballer is a decided loss to Edinburgh football. The popularity of Burns manifested itself in the huge gathering that congregated at Mount Vernon Cemetery on the day of his burial, when he was laid to rest beside his sweetheart, who also met her death in the regrettable accident.

The defeats against Third Lanark and Aberdeen have brought down our League stock rather badly, but we must make amends for these poor returns in our October engagements.

The poor and disjointed form of our forwards is chiefly to blame for the loss of these valuable points. It must be understood, however, that their efforts were not blessed with the best of luck, for, in both games, there were several occasions when the crossbar or a lucky foot prevented the ball entering the net.

The famous Celtic side are our visitors to-day, and they make no secret of the fact that, like ourselves, they must restore themselves in the eyes of their supporters. Our front rank has again been remodelled with a view to greater efficiency, and we hope the efforts of our enthusiastic and capable rear lined will be turned to better account by the front-rankers.

The "A" team play the return match with the Celtic second string at Parkhead to-day, and judging by the good form served up by both sides last week a rousing encounter should be the outcome.

Magnus M'Phee, the junior Edina player, made quite an auspicious start in senior football by scoring two goals last Saturday.

We have transferred W. S. Chalmers and L. Macmillan to Manchester United and Partick Thistle respectively. Negotiations in the transfers of the players were carried through on Thursday of this week. We wish them both the best of luck in their new spheres.

Hearts programme editorial in October 1932. The team finished third in the League and clearly benefited from the methods of new trainer James Kerr, who arrived from Rangers. The team also reached the Scottish Cup Semi-finals, but went down 2-1 to Celtic after a replay.

International goalkeeper, Jack Harkness, who was recruited from Queen's Park in May 1928 and was Hearts' last line of defence until he retired in 1936 due to a recurring leg injury. The agile and brave custodian won eight of his eleven international caps while at Tynecastle.

The scene at McLeod Street before the Scottish Cup Third Round match against Rangers on Wednesday 21 February 1934. A Tynecastle midweek-record attendance of 48, 895 saw Hearts go down 2-1, although one of the Rangers' goals was lucky to stand after a handball and offside claim by the home defenders.

Andy Anderson, one of Scotland's finest defenders, joined Hearts from Bailleston Juniors in 1929. This resolute full-back played for his country on twenty-three occasions and had the honour of captaining Hearts and Scotland over many years. He retired during the early years of the Second World War.

Hearts' new striker Dave McCulloch goes close with a header during the 1-0 victory over Airdrie at Tynecastle in September 1934.

Hearts' dashing centre forward, Dave McCulloch, who was signed from Third Lanark in June 1934 for £530. He had a brilliant first season and topped the League scoring charts with thirty-eight goals. His goals took Hearts to third place in the League and it came as no surprise when the international striker was transferred to Brentford in 1935 for the substantial fee of £5,500.

Hearts in the 1933/34 season.
From left to right, back row: Alex Massie,
Andy Herd, Andy Anderson, Jack Harkness,
Tom O'Neil, John Johnstone. Front row: Bob
Johnstone, Tommy Walker, Archie Gardiner,
John Smith, Willie Murray.

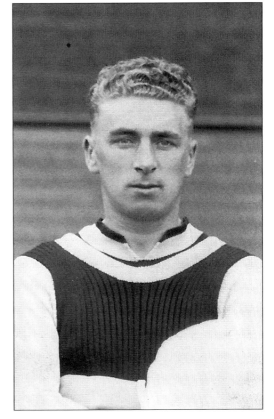

Alex Massie, a midfield genius for Hearts. He
was signed in September 1930 from Dolphin
FC (Dublin), although he was registered with
Bury FC who claimed £710 from Hearts.
Alex, who also appeared for Bethlehem Steel
FC in the USA, played for Scotland eleven
times while at Tynecastle and primed the
Hearts attack until 1935, when he was sold
to Aston Villa for £5,500.

Willie Reid, Hearts' Northern Irish internationalist, halts the Airdrie attack at Tynecastle in September 1934. Willie was one of the men who inspired Hearts to the Scottish Cup Semifinals in the Spring of 1935, but the 'Maroons' went down 2-0 to Rangers after a replay.

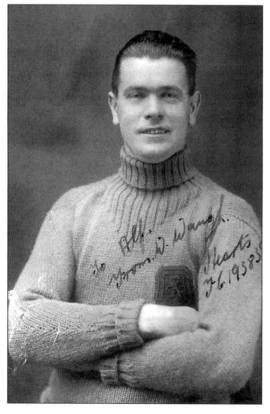

Willie Waugh, a solid and reliable goalkeeper, who was signed from Durhamtown Rangers in December 1928. He was loaned to Third Lanark and Hibs early in his career, but returned to keep Hearts' goal from 1936 to 1941. He was good enough to win a full international cap against Czechoslovakia in December 1937.

Dave McCulloch challenges the Dunfermline defence at Tynecastle in August 1935. The match was drawn 1-1 and Hearts went on to have a disappointing season, finishing fifth in the League and losing to Third Lanark in the First Round of the Scottish Cup.

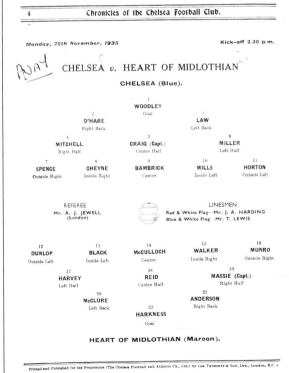

Monday, 25th November, 1935   Kick-off 2.30 p.m.

AWAY

CHELSEA v. HEART OF MIDLOTHIAN

CHELSEA (Blue).

1
WOODLEY
Goal

2   3
O'HARE   LAW
Right Back   Left Back

4   5   6
MITCHELL   CRAIG (Capt.)   MILLER
Right Half   Centre Half   Left Half

7   8   9   10   11
SPENCE   CHEYNE   BAMBRICK   MILLS   HORTON
Outside Right Inside Right Centre Inside Left Outside Left

REFEREE   LINESMEN
Mr. A. J. JEWELL   Red & White Flag—Mr. J. A. HARDING
(London)   Blue & White Flag—Mr. T. LEWIS

12   13   14   15   16
DUNLOP   BLACK   McCULLOCH   WALKER   MUNRO
Outside Left Inside Left Centre. Inside Right Outside Right

17   18   19
HARVEY   REID   MASSIE (Capt.)
Left Half   Centre Half   Right Half

20   21
McCLURE   ANDERSON
Left Back   Right Back

22
HARKNESS
Goal

HEART OF MIDLOTHIAN (Maroon).

Printed and Published for the Proprietors (The Chelsea Football and Athletic Co., Ltd.) by Jas. Truscott & Son, Ltd., London, E.C.

The Chelsea FC programme anticipates the teams for Hearts friendly in London in November 1935. Andy Black and Dave McCulloch scored in Hearts' 2-0 victory.

59

Hearts pressurize the Dunfermline defence at Tynecastle in August 1935.

Freddie Warren, a tricky left-winger who was signed from Middlesbrough in May 1936 for £650. He is the only Tynecastle man to have been capped by Wales and starred in Hearts' great forward line – Briscoe, Walker, Garrett, Black and Warren. In the 1936/37 season he could not inspire Hearts to a higher place than fifth in the League. The players did run up a 15-0 victory against King's Park in the Scottish Cup, but success slipped away in the next round at Hamilton.

Charlie Wipfler, who came from Bristol City, scores with a diving header against Partick Thistle in August 1935. He also scored twice in Hearts 8-3 demolition of Hibs, in a League match played at Tynecastle in September of that year.

Hearts' new manager David Pratt replaced William McCartney in July 1935. The former Notts County boss brought the 'tracksuit' style of management to Tynecastle at long last.

Andy Black scores in Hearts' 4-1 victory over Queen's Park in December 1935.

HEARTS 5 "CAPS" 1935

Hearts five internationalists in 1935 with chairman Alex Irvine. The Tynecastle stars, from left to right, are: Andy Anderson, Tommy Walker, Dave McCulloch, Sandy Herd and Alex Massie. Hearts' management failed to harness the individual qualities of many fine players who appeared in maroon during the 1930s.

Andy Black, a stylish striker who was recruited in 1934 from Shawfield Juniors. The international marksman hit 124 League goals for the club before moving to Manchester City in June 1946 for £4,000.

Tommy Walker, whose creative skills were unsurpassed in Britain during the 1930s. He was taken onto the Tynecastle ground staff in February 1932 and signed professionally in May that year after a spell with Linlithgow Rose. Tommy won the first of twenty caps at the age of nineteen and he also appeared in five League and eleven wartime internationals. The dynamic midfielder was transferred to Chelsea in September 1946 for £6,000.

Hearts in 1937/38, now under the management of former Arsenal and England goalkeeper Frank Moss. League form was much improved and the club finished as runners-up to Celtic in the Championship. Unfortunately, the 'Maroons' were bundled out of the Scottish Cup by Second Division Dundee United.

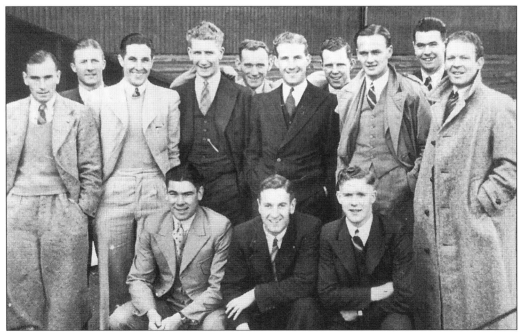

Hearts players pictured at Middlesbrough in March 1939. The League challenge failed to materialize and the 'Maroons' finished fourth in the season before the Second World War. In the Scottish Cup, Hearts defeated Penicuik Athletic 14-2 and Elgin City 14-1 before Celtic ended the run with a controversial 2-1 win in a Third Round replay in Glasgow.

Tommy Walker scores the only goal of the England versus Scotland match at Wembley in 1938.

Five

War Again and Beyond

HEART OF MIDLOTHIAN FOOTBALL CLUB LIMITED

TELEPHONE 61321

MANAGER: D. M'LEAN

TYNECASTLE PARK, GORGIE ROAD
EDINBURGH, 11

Dear Sir,

Match Versus..

on Saturday........................*19*........*at*..................

meet at...................................*kick-off*.................

Bus
———— leaves...*at*.........
Train

If unable to play please advise me at once.

Yours truly,

D. mcLean

Manager.

This advice note was issued to players who were selected to play for Hearts during the Second World War. When war was declared in September 1939, the Scottish League was abandoned after only five matches. A month later, two Leagues of sixteen clubs were organized with Hearts playing in the East and North Division. Wages were restricted to £2 per week.

AIR RAID WARNING

All persons admitted to this ground should, in the interest of Public Safety

CARRY A GAS MASK.

In the event of an Air Raid Warning, football play will be suspended immediately. All Exit Gates from the Stands and Ground will be opened.

You should take cover underneath the Stands or against the Barricade and Embankment.

KEEP CALM.

REMEMBER—

You are safer in the accommodation provided in this ground than in the street.

You should not leave the ground unless you can reach your home or an Air Raid Shelter within a few minutes.

If you wish to leave the ground, please do so in a quiet and orderly manner. Having taken cover, wait for the "All Clear" Signal to be sounded.

The Air Raid Warning for spectators watching Hearts tussle with Falkirk for the East and North Division Championship. The 'Maroons' finished runners-up, although the team scored 104 goals. Tynecastle's capacity was restricted to 8,000 in the 1939/40 season and the average gate was 3,452.

Hearts players enjoy some golf early on during the Second World War. Soon the regulars would join the Armed Forces and the team would be made up from guests, soldiers on leave, youngsters, and players in reserved occupations. Hearts joined the Southern League in 1940/41 and finished tenth.

The club was still able to pay a dividend to shareholders in July 1941. This was largely due to a splendid run in the Southern League Cup, where Hearts faced Rangers in the final at Hampden before 68,000 fans. The match was tied 1-1 and the Glasgow side won the replay 4-2. Hearts also reached the Semi-finals of the Summer Cup that season, but went down 4-2, again to Rangers.

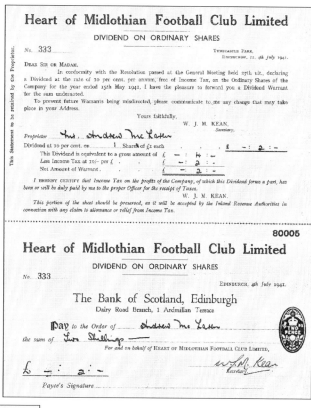

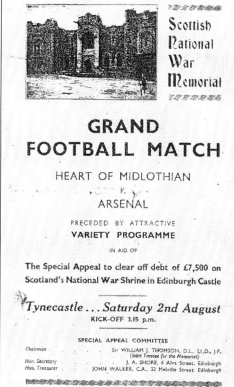

The programme cover for one of the many fund-raising events supported by the club during the War. Hearts lost this match 1-0 to Arsenal in August 1941. The team was now managed by David McLean, who saw his new side finish fifth in the Southern League in 1941/42.

Hearts stalwarts during the early years of the Second World War. Left to right: George Robson, Alex Hyslop, Alf Pope, Tommy Walker and Tommy Brown.

Alf Pope (left), a redoubtable full-back who was signed from Halifax Town in February 1937 for £600. The tough Yorkshireman served in the RAF during the war, but came up to Edinburgh as often as he could to pull on a maroon shirt. However, Alfie mostly played in the colours of Blackpool during these difficult years.

Dominating centre half Jimmy Dykes was recruited in May 1933 from Law Juveniles. The giant defender was a first team regular at nineteen and earned two international caps before the war. Jimmy represented his country in four wartime internationals before joining the RAF and then going to work in the Belfast shipyards. He left Tynecastle in the 1942/43 season and, without his strength, Hearts finished seventh in the Southern League.

HEART OF MIDLOTHIAN FOOTBALL CLUB · LIMITED

PHONE: 61321.

MANAGER
D. McLEAN

SECRETARY
W. J. M. KEAN, C.A.

REGISTERED ADDRESS:
TYNECASTLE PARK · GORGIE ROAD

EDINBURGH·11 ___18th May___1944

Mr Willier MacAndrew,
121 St Vincent Street,
Glasgow.

Dear Mr MacAndrew,
            I have received retain and transfer list to-day
I have omitted two Amateurs. George Cown and James Watters which
you might add to your list if it is not too late.
John McL Campbell should read Am instead of Prov and Robert B. S. Lamb
and Wm A. C. Mitchell should read Prov.

yours sincerely,

D McLean

Manager David McLean started to restructure the team during the 1943/44 season and Hearts improved to finish fourth. Apart from the players, already mentioned, he introduced Tam MacKenzie, Jimmy Brown, Archie Kelly, Alex McCrae and Willie McFarlane. Icelandic amateur Otto Jonsson became the first foreign player to wear maroon.

Bob Baxter, a skilled and inspirational centre half who won international honours while at Middlesbrough. Bob played for Hearts in the 1939/40 season, when he returned to Edinburgh to work at Gilmerton pit, and also appeared in two wartime internationals. Bob was then snatched by Hibs, but returned to Tynecastle in 1945 to play an important role in developing the Hearts youngsters.

The famous Alfie Conn made the breakthrough in the 1944/45 season after being signed from Inveresk Thistle. Although Hearts were only fifth in the Southern League that year, the form of the club's youngsters was very promising. Archie Kelly, for example, was Scotland's top League scorer with thirty-three goals, including seven in a 10-3 victory over Albion Rovers.

SOUVENIR PROGRAMME

COMBINED SERVICES (GERMANY) XI
VERSUS
HEART OF MIDLOTHIAN F. C.
AT
HIGHBURY STADIUM, CELLE
SUNDAY, 2nd JUNE 1946 at 15.00 HRS.

COMBINED SERVICES XI

BLY
(Hull City)

COUTLAND   RICKABY
(Sunderland)   (Middlesborough)

WILLIAMS   COMPTON   HODGKINSON
(Chester)   (Arsenal & England)   (Leeds United)

STEVENS   LEWIS   STEELE   ROBERTS
(Fulham)   (Arsenal & England)   (Morton)   (Derby County)

DAVIES
(Sunderland)

Referee: Capt. Howell
(B. A. O. R.)

J. WALKER McCRAE KELLY T. WALKER McFARLANE
NEILSON   BAXTER   COX
JOHNSTON   McARA
BROWN

HEART OF MIDLOTHIAN F. C.

**A COLLECTION WILL BE TAKEN AT THE GAME
IN AID OF ST. DUNSTAN'S FUND
PLEASE GIVE GENEROUSLY**

The war in Europe finished in May 1945 and many clubs took part in exhibition matches to entertain the troops stationed overseas. In this game Tommy Walker scored twice to earn Hearts a 3-2 victory before 8,000 servicemen. Hearts were seventh in the League in the 1945/46 season and reached the Southern League Cup Semi-finals.

Hearts' immediate post-war team. Football had returned to familiar lines in the 1946/47 season with the return of the Scottish League Championship, the Scottish FA Cup and a new competition, the Scottish League Cup. The young Tynecastle team were fourth in the League and were hustled out of the Scottish Cup by Second ('B') Division Arbroath. The 'Maroons' also went down 6-2 to Aberdeen in the League Cup Semi-finals.

Classy striker George Hamilton was signed in December 1947 from Aberdeen in exchange for Archie Kelly and £8,000. Unfortunately, the international forward, who scored forty goals in forty–three wartime appearances for the club, could not settle in Edinburgh and returned to the 'Dons' in June 1948 for a fee of £12,000.

Arthur Dixon cost Hearts £5,000 when he was transferred from Clyde in September 1947. The club had spent lavishly on Dixon, George Hamilton and Bobby Flavell, but there was no immediate payback with the team finishing ninth in the League and making no impact in the cup competitions.

Hearts in 1949. From left to right, back row: Charlie Cox, Bobby Parker, Jimmy Brown, Bobby Dougan, Tam MacKenzie, Davie Laing. Front row: Tommy Sloan, Alfie Conn, Willie Bauld, Jimmy Wardhaugh, Archie Williams. Although Hearts were only eighth in the League in 1948/49, average attendances reached a peak of 28,196. This was not only due to the post-war boom, but clear evidence of the success of David McLean's youth policy which had been boosted by the appointment of Tommy Walker as assistant manager in January 1949.

The Hearts defence in rare action against Falkirk at Tynecastle in November 1949. The 'Maroons' won 9-0, sparking off a Championship challenge. However, the team finished in third place and were fourth in the 1950/51 season.

Bobby Flavell was a dynamic winger or centre forward who cost Hearts a Scottish-record fee of £10,000 when he was recruited from Airdrieonians in December 1947. The international front man could have been the ideal feeder to the 'terrible trio', had he not decided to join Millionarios FC of Bogota in June 1950. He was reputed to earn ten times more than Hearts' basic wage of £12 per week.

Hearts in 1952. From left to right, back row: D. McLeod (Assistant Trainer), R. Parker, R. Dougan, W. Watters, J. Milne, T. MacKenzie, D. Laing, J. Harvey. Front row: J. Durkin, J. Cumming, W. Bauld, J. Wardhaugh, J. Urquhart. Hearts were fourth in the League and Scottish Cup Semi-finalists in both the 1951/52 and 1952/53 seasons. Sadly, David McLean died in February 1951 and would not see the results of his efforts for the club.

Hearts legend John Cumming was signed from Carluke Rovers in January 1950. At half-back or on the wing, he had established his place by the 1953/54 season, when Hearts were runners-up in the League Championship. John played 613 games for Hearts and was the driving force behind the club's success in two League Championships, four League Cup Finals and one Scottish Cup Final. He also played nine times for Scotland.

Six

The Fabulous Fifties

Willie Bauld opens the scoring in the League Cup Final in October 1954. The 'King' scored a hat-trick, with Jimmy Wardhaugh adding another in Hearts 4-2 victory over Motherwell.

Jimmy Wardhaugh, Bobby Paker and Willie Bauld celebrate with a drink from the League Cup, the first trophy won by the club since 1906.

Hearts bring back the League Cup to Edinburgh in 1954.
The winning heroes were: Willie Duff, Bobby Parker (Captain), Tam MacKenzie, Dave Mackay, Freddie Glidden, John Cumming, Jim Souness, Alfie Conn, Willie Bauld, Jimmy Wardhaugh and Johnny Urquhart.

An Aberdeen defender defies the Tynecastle attack in 1955. Johnny Hamilton, Jimmy Wardhaugh and Alex Young are the Hearts men in the centre of the picture. Hearts were fourth in the League in the 1954/55 season.

Willie Bauld scores against Rangers in the Scottish Cup Quarter-final tie at Tynecastle in March 1956. Hearts won 4-0 and marched into the final by defeating Raith Rovers in the penultimate round.

SCOTTISH CUP
WINNERS

HAMPDEN PARK
APRIL 1956

DUFF

KIRK   MACKENZIE

MACKAY   GLIDDEN   CUMMING

YOUNG   CONN   BAULD   WARDHAUGH   CRAWFORD

The famous faces that brought the Scottish Cup back to Tynecastle in April 1956 for a fifth time. Celtic were defeated 3-1 in the final, thanks to glory goals from Ian Crawford (2) and Alfie Conn. The attendance was the largest-ever to have watched a Hearts match –133,399 – and there were 60,000 supporting the 'Maroons'.

The Board of Directors, Manager, Players, Trainers and Staff of The Heart of Midlothian Football Club desire to express their appreciation of the kind congratulations which have been so warmly extended to them on the occasion of their winning the Scottish Cup. This happy result has been made possible by the loyal support and constant encouragement of their many friends.

TYNECASTLE PARK
EDINBURGH

April 1956

Huge celebrations followed Hearts' victory in the Scottish Cup and the club made sure that all the good wishes which flooded into Tynecastle were acknowledged.

Alfie Conn scores Hearts' third goal in the 1956 Scottish Cup Final against Celtic. The winning team was: Willie Duff, Bobby Kirk, Tam MacKenzie, Dave Mackay, Freddie Glidden, John Cumming, Alex Young, Alfie Conn, Willie Bauld, Jimmy Wardhaugh and Ian Crawford.

Hearts' star-studded attack, including the 'Terrible Trio' of Conn, Bauld and Wardhaugh. These magnificent players first came together in October 1948. At the end of their careers, Alfie Conn had scored 219 goals, Willie Bauld 356 goals and Jimmy Wardhaugh 375 goals.

After finishing as runners-up in the 1956/57 season, Hearts were imperious in 1957/58, winning the Championship by a margin of thirteen points from Rangers. From left to right, back row: P. Smith, A. Findlay, H. Goldie, G. Dobie, T. MacKenzie, G. Marshall, T. Brown, J. Howieson, G. Campbell, W. Higgins, J. Thomson. Middle row: D. McLeod, R. Parker, A. Bowman, J. Milne, J. Murray, D. Mackay, W. Lindores, R. Kirk, G. Thomson , J. Cumming, J. Harvey. Front row: R. Paton, A. Conn, A. Young, J. Wardhaugh, W. Bauld, J. Foley, J. Crawford, J. Hamilton, J. McFadzean.

An unusual view of the Hearts squad which earned the club its third League Championship with a new points record of sixty-two.

In winning the 1957/58 Championship, Hearts also set a new goalscoring record for the top division – 132 in thirty-four games. The picture shows Jimmy Wardhaugh scoring against Raith Rovers on 29 March 1958 and breaking Motherwell's previous record of 119 League goals in a season.

The League Championship souvenir pennant from 1957/58.

A goalmouth incident involving Jimmy Murray against a Scotland XI in March 1958. The match was arranged to assist Scotland's preparation for the World Cup Finals, but the national team went down 3-2 to the country's finest club side. This encounter was played under the Tynecastle floodlights, which had been inaugurated in October 1957.

Hearts' Championship squad leaves for North America in 1958. Since the war, Hearts had also been to Germany, Sweden and South Africa.

Hearts apply pressure against Standard Liege in the club's first-ever European tie. Although the 'Maroons' won the home leg 2-1, the players found the 5-1 deficit from the away leg in Liege just too much. Hearts have now played forty-eight European matches, appearing in all three major competitions.

Dave Mackay and Jimmy Murray challenge the Raith Rovers goalkeeper. Both played for Scotland in the 1958 World Cup Finals in Sweden and both were inspirational in the 1958/59 season when Hearts only failed to retain the Championship by two points. If the team had won on the final day of the season against Celtic the title would have remained in Gorgie.

Airdrie goalkeeper Jock Wallace is beaten by a flashing shot at Tynecastle. Wallace would eventually become coach and then assistant manager of Hearts.

Smith of Partick Thistle scores with a header in the League Cup Final at Hampden in October 1958. Despite this, Hearts crushed the Glasgow team 5-1 with goals from Bauld (2), Murray (2) and Johnny Hamilton.

Dave Mackay, Jimmy Murray, Willie Bauld and Ian Crawford enjoy a celebration drink after the League Cup Final victory in 1958. Hearts' heroes were: Marshall, Kirk, Thomson, Mackay (Captain), Glidden, Cumming, Hamilton, Murray, Bauld, Wardhaugh and Crawford.

Hearts leave for the summer tour of Australia in 1959. Manager Tommy Walker (standing on the extreme left) had led the club back to the forefront of Scottish football.

HEART OF MIDLOTHIAN
FOOTBALL CLUB

Tour of

AUSTRALIA

✿ ✿ ✿

May—June 1959

✿ ✿ ✿

ITINERARY

The players' itinerary for the Australian Tour, during which Hearts played fifteen matches, winning fourteen and scoring 109 goals.

Alex Young scores against Celtic in August 1959.

Hearts retained the League Cup in October 1959 with a 2-1 victory over Third Lanark in the final at Hampden Park. Here, Alex Young scores the winning goal in the fifty-ninth minute.

Third Lanark took the lead in the 1959 League Cup Final, but a brilliant long-range drive by Johnny Hamilton equalised for Hearts after fifty-seven minutes (above). The winning Tynecastle side was: Gordon Marshall, Bobby Kirk, George Thomson, Andy Bowman, John Cumming (Captain), Billy Higgins, Gordon Smith, Ian Crawford, Alex Young, Bobby Blackwood and Johnny Hamilton.

In the 1959/60 season, Hearts won the League Championship for the fourth time in the club's history. The title was secured by a 4-4 draw at Paisley in the penultimate game. Here, Alex Young scores Hearts' third goal on this exciting occasion.

Seven

Hearts in the Sixties and Seventies

Winners of the League Championship and the League Cup in the 1959/60 season . From left to right, back row: Andy Bowman, Bobby Kirk, Wilson Brown, Billy Higgins, Willie Bauld. Middle row: Donald McLeod, George Thomson, Gordon Smith, Gordon Marshall, Andy Fraser, Jim McFadzean, Jimmy Murray, John Harvey. Front row: Ian Crawford, Alex Young, Jimmy Milne, Tommy Walker, John Cumming, Bobby Blackwood, Johnny Hamilton.

Tynecastle Park in 1960, showing the new covered enclosure on the distillery side, which was erected the previous year.

Hearts in 1962. From left to right, back row: Davie Holt, Bobby Kirk, Gordon Marshall, Willie Polland, Billy Higgins, Willie Wallace. Front row: Jim Rodger, Danny Paton, Bobby Ross, John Cumming, Bobby Blackwood. Hearts failed to make an impact in the League during the early 1960s, but reached the League Cup Final in October 1961. After a 1-1 draw, Hearts went down 3-1 in the replay to Rangers.

Willie Hamilton scores his first goal for Hearts against Dundee at Tynecastle in September 1962. This gifted footballer had been recruited three months earlier from Middlesbrough for a fee of only £3,000. It was his skill that fired Hearts and Willie became immensely popular with the fans.

The one and only Willie Hamilton, who inspired Hearts to a fourth League Cup Final victory in October 1962. It was his penetrating run and cross that set up the only goal of the match against Kilmarnock, the scorer being Norrie Davidson. Hearts' team was: Marshall, Polland, Holt, Cumming, Barry, Higgins, Wallace, Paton, Davidson, W. Hamilton and J. Hamilton.

Davie Holt, Hearts' international left-back who played 350 games for the club between 1960 and 1969. The rugged defender was one of the bitterly disappointed Hearts squad that lost the League Championship on goal average to Kilmarnock in 1964/65.

The legendary Sir Stanley Matthews is tracked by Davie Holt at Tynecastle in 1964. Stoke City beat Hearts 2-1.

The Hearts squad which lost the 1964/65 Championship on the final day of the League season. Kilmarnock took the title on the old goal average system after winning 2-0 at Tynecastle on that fateful day. Both clubs had fifty points but, by dividing goals against into goals for, 'Killie' took the title by .04.

Willie Wallace scores against Rangers in the League Cup at Tynecastle in August 1965. Wallace was a remarkable striker who hit 158 goals for Hearts after signing from Raith Rovers in April 1961. The international striker moved to Celtic in December 1966 for a fee of £29,000.

Willie Wallace is on the mark against Maccabi Tel Aviv in August 1966. Within a few months it was all-change at Tynecastle with John Harvey taking over as manager from Tommy Walker and Wallace heading for Celtic Park.

Another goal for Willie Wallace, this time against Celtic in the Scottish Cup at Tynecastle in March 1966. The game finished 3-3 and was watched by a massive crowd of 45,965. Celtic won the replay 3-1 before a remarkable 72,000 spectators, including 10,000 Tynecastle fans.

Hearts' Norwegian international forward Roald Jensen scores against Aberdeen in October 1967. Although League form had been poor, Hearts stormed through to the final with Roald Jensen scoring from the penalty spot to eventually defeat Morton in the Semi-final replay.

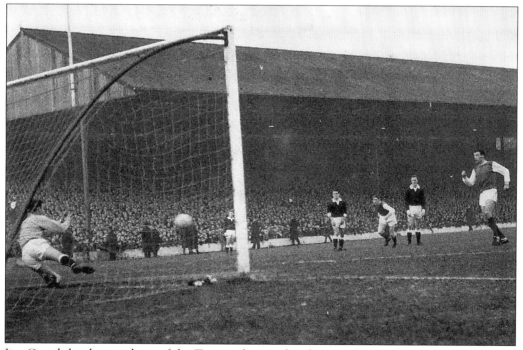

Jim Cruickshank was a hero of the Tynecastle crowd and is seen here saving a penalty from Joe Davis of Hibs in January 1967. The international 'keeper also blocked two rebounds after this kick, to ecstatic applause from the terraces.

From left to right: Donald Ford, John Cumming, George Miller, Tommy Traynor, Jim Townsend and Arthur Mann prepare for the 1968 Scottish Cup Final. Unfortunately, Hearts could not master Dunfermline and lost 3-1.

Roald Jensen, a skilled and pacey forward with an individual style which sometimes irritated the Hearts management. He was signed from Brann SK in December 1964 and made 126 appearances, scoring twenty-seven goals before returning to Bergen in 1971. This superb entertainer was capped by Norway during his stay at Tynecastle, a rare event at this time.

Hearts in 1970. From left to right, back row: Ian Sneddon, Dave Clunie, Alan Anderson, Kenny Garland, Jim Cruickshank, Tommy Vietch, George Fleming, Jim Brown, Donald Ford. Front row: Ernie Winchester, Wilson Wood, Jim Townsend, Eddie Thomson, Kevin Hegarty, Roald Jensen, Andy Lynch, Peter Oliver. Hearts' domestic form was poor during the early 1970s, but there were many stirring moments in the Texaco Cup.

Although seasons 1968/69 and 1969/70 were disappointing for Hearts, goalkeeper Jim Cruickshank gave supreme performances and saved the club's reputation on many occasions. He joined the club in May 1960 from Queen's Park and went on to make a remarkable 610 appearances for Hearts. Tragically, Jim won no club honours during his time at Tynecastle.

The programme from the Texaco Cup Final in May 1971, when Hearts met Wolves. A crowd of 25,027 saw Wolves win the first-leg at Tynecastle by 3-1, but Hearts restored some pride with a 1-0 victory at Molineux, thanks to a George Fleming goal.

Tommy Murray attacks the Hibs defence at Easter Road in 1972. Bobby Seith had taken over as manager in 1970 and this unusual strip was introduced under his command. It failed to inspire Hearts and the club even suffered its record defeat on New Years' Day 1973 (0-7 versus Hibs).

Hearts squad in the centenary year of 1974, when the team reached the Scottish Cup Semi-finals. This was virtually the same squad that helped the club to qualify for the new Premier Division in the 1974/75 season, under the new management of John Hagart. From left to right, back row: Donald Ford, Ian Sneddon, Dave Clunie, Kenny Garland, Alan Anderson, Jim Jefferies, Eric Carruthers. Front row: Kenny Aird, John Stevenson, Drew Busby, Jimmy Brown, Bobby Prentice, Tommy Murray, Jimmy Cant.

Hearts squad in 1975/76, when the team finished fifth in the new Premier Division. The 'Maroons' also reached the Scottish Cup Final but went down 3-1 to Rangers.

Nr. 8   20.10.1976

Heart of Midlothian F. C.

Hintere Reihe von links: John Gallagher, John Hay, Jim Cruickshank, Roy Kay, Cammy Fraser;

mittlere Reihe von links: Jimmy Brown, Ralph Callaghan, Sandy Burrell, Don Murray, Jim Jefferies, Dave Clunie;

vordere Reihe von links: Willie Gibson, Kenny Aird, Graham Shaw, Manager John Hagart, Drew Busby, Donald Park, Rab Prentice.

Die „Hearts" sind in Heimspielen ziemlich herzlos

Die zweite Runde des Europapokals der Pokalsieger bringt für den HSV eine ungleich schwerere Aufgabe als bei der Premiere gegen den isländischen Vertreter I. F. Keflavik. Unsere Mannschaft ist gewarnt, die kampfstarke Elf von Heart of Midlothian darf auf keinen Fall unterschätzt werden. Es gilt einen beruhigenden Vorsprung herauszuschießen. Denn in ihrer schottischen Heimat, in der Hauptstadt Edinburgh, sind die Hearts nur schwer zu bezwingen. Diese Erfahrung mußte der 1. SC Lokomotive Leipzig machen, als er im Hinspiel 2:0 gegen die Hearts gewann, als Favorit nach Schottland flog, dann aber im Sturmwirbel des Gegners gleich 1:5 unterging. Die begeisterungsfähigen schottischen Fans sind praktisch der 12. Spieler, so stark sind sie in ihrer Unterstützung. Die HSV-Anhänger sollten zeigen, daß man auch in Hamburg hinter seiner Mannschaft steht. Gerade in einer Zeit, in der unser Team auch ohne Nogly, Memering und Keller alles gibt, um ein Publikumsmagnet zu bleiben. Unsere Elf wird die Unterstützung der Zuschauer mit einer starken Leistung honorieren.

HSV EUROPA-POKAL Heart of Midlothian Edinburgh Schottischer Pokalsieger Mittwoch · 20. Oktober · 19³⁰ Uhr.

The programme for the Hamburg versus Hearts match in the Second Round of the Cup Winners Cup. After losing the European tie 8-3 on aggregate, Hearts reached the League Cup and Scottish Cup Semi-finals. The season then collapsed and in April 1977 the club was relegated for the first time in its history.

The squad which immediately won promotion from the First Division in 1977/78, under new manager Willie Ormond. From left to right, back row: Jack Smyth, Ian Black, Stuart Cribbes, Jim Jefferies, Graham Shaw, John Gallacher, David Johnston, Donald McLaren. Front row: Lawrie Tierney, Walter Kidd, Eamonn Bannon, Malcolm Robertson, Rab Prentice, Donald Park, Willie Gibson, Cammy Fraser.

Willie Gibson scores with a penalty against Hibs in March 1979, during a game that ended 1-1. This was one of the highlights of a dismal campaign which saw Hearts relegated for a second time in three years.

Eight

The Eighties

Now under the management of Bobby Moncur, Hearts won the First Division Championship in the 1979/80 season. The title was secured on the last day of the campaign when Frank Liddell scored the only goal of the match against Airdrie at Tynecastle.

Frank Liddell, Jim Jefferies and Graham Shaw – heroes of the First Division Championship success in 1980.

Willie Gibson pressurizes the Stirling Albion defence at Annfield. He had been a prolific scorer for nearly ten years, but his goals dried up in the 1980/81 season, when Hearts were again relegated.

In June 1981, Wallace Mercer became Hearts' majority shareholder and a brave new era opened for the club. Tony Ford became manager and a record fee of £155,000 was paid to Dundee United for Willie Pettigrew and Derek Addison. However, the team struggled and popular player/coach Alex Macdonald took over as manager in February 1982. This was too late to secure promotion.

Willie Pettigrew scores his second goal in Hearts 7-1 hammering of Clyde in the 1982/83 League Cup. Willie scored four goals that afternoon and assisted the club to the Semi-finals, where the 'Maroons' went down 4-1 to Rangers on aggregate.

Player/manager Alex Macdonald celebrates his winning goal against Motherwell in August 1982. Alex brought his old Ibrox colleagues Sandy Jardine and Willie Johnston to Tynecastle, while he also gave a regular opportunity to youngsters Davie Bowman, Gary Mackay and John Robertson. He was rewarded with promotion back to the Premier Division.

Gary Mackay scores from the penalty spot in Hearts' 2-0 victory over Airdrie in April 1983.

Jimmy Bone scores the winning goal in Hearts' 3-2 victory over Hibs in September 1983. This was the most exciting campaign for many years and ended with Hearts securing fifth place in the Premier Division and qualifying for the UEFA Cup.

Hearts secured a UEFA Cup place after drawing 1-1 with Celtic at Tynecastle in May 1984. The goalscorer was Willie Johnston who takes the congratulations of his colleagues.

A pennant issued in connection with Hearts visit to France in September 1984 to play Paris St Germain in the UEFA Cup. The 'Maroons' lost 4-0 but restored some pride with a 2-2 draw in the return leg at Tynecastle.

Tynecastle in the mid-1980s.

Jimmy Bone scores Hearts 6,000th League goal in the match against Dundee United at Tannadice in December 1984. The team finished seventh in the League and reached the League Cup Semi-finals that season.

Gary Mackay scores against Dundee in February 1985.

Two Hearts legends – Gary Mackay (back) and John Robertson (front). Industrious midfielder Gary Mackay played a club record of 737 first team matches and represented Scotland on four occasions. John Robertson scored a club record 214 League goals and a magnificent total of 310 in 720 games; John represented Scotland on sixteen occasions.

New recruit John Colquhoun scores a fine goal against Celtic in August 1985. This was the opening game in an outstanding season in which Hearts finished as runners-up in the Premier Division and reached the Scottish Cup Final.

John Colquhoun scores in the 1-1 draw against Aberdeen in April 1986. Hearts won the following game against Clydebank and only needed a draw in the final game of the season to secure the Championship. Tragically, Hearts went down 2-0 to Dundee and Celtic took the title on goal difference.

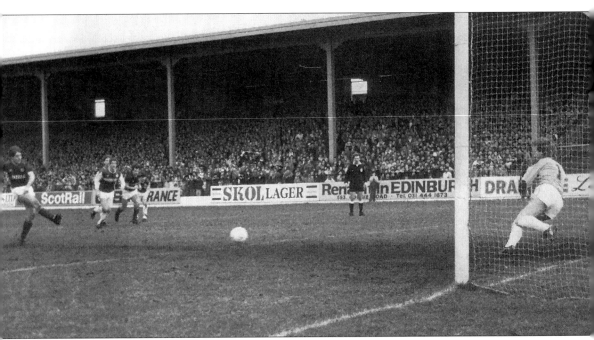

John Robertson nets a penalty against Hibs in March 1986. This was one of his record twenty-seven goals against the Leith team in derby matches.

Ian Jardine heads home against Dundee in October 1985. The match ended 1-1 but this was the first of thirty-one unbeaten games which took Hearts to the brink of a glory 'double'.

Hearts attack the Dukla goal in the UEFA Cup tie at Prague in October 1986. The home side won 1-0 and went through on away goals after their 3-2 defeat at Tynecastle.

Hearts' classy international sweeper Craig Levein, who suffered a serious knee injury in the early months of the 1986/87 season. Without his services, Hearts finished fifth in the League and lost to St Mirren in the Scottish Cup Semi-finals.

John Robertson scores during Hearts 4-2 victory over Dundee in October 1987. The 'Maroons' were runners-up in the Premier Division in 1987/88 and reached the Scottish Cup Semi-finals, only to lose to a last-minute goal from Celtic.

Hearts' impressive support at Tolka Park, Dublin, where St Patrick's Athletic were beaten 2-0 in the UEFA Cup in September 1988.

Tynecastle Park in the late 1980s – time for an improvement.

Iain Ferguson in the UEFA Cup Quarter-final tie against Bayern Munich at Tynecastle. Hearts won 1-0 thanks to a goal scored by Ferguson, but lost the return leg at the Olympic Stadium by 2-0 in March 1989.

Henry Smith, an ever-present during the 1988/89 season, when Hearts were sixth in the League and reached the League Cup Semi-final. Henry was a fine 'keeper who in fourteen years' service recorded 214 shut-outs in 598 competitive matches. He represented Scotland on three occasions.

Walter Kidd challenges the Celtic 'keeper Pat Bonner in December 1989 during a 0-0 draw. Hearts finished third in the Premier Division that season.

Nine

The Nineties

Scott Crabbe pressurizes Celtic in April 1991. Hearts were fifth in the League under new manager Joe Jordan.

Tynecastle in the early 1990s.

John Robertson stretches the Motherwell defence. John's twenty goals helped Hearts to runners-up position in the Premier Division in the 1991/92 season. The 'Maroons' also reached the Scottish Cup Semi-finals but lost on penalties to Airdrie.

The Hearts BP Youth Cup-winning team in 1993.

Ian Baird comes close with a header against Dundee United in August 1992. Hearts were fifth in the League in the 1992/93 season and reached the Scottish-Cup Semi-finals, where the 'Maroons' lost 2-1 to Rangers at Celtic Park.

Redevelopment of Tynecastle commences at the end of the 1993/94 season.

Wayne Foster scores the winning goal in the Scottish Cup Fourth Round tie against Hibs at Easter Road in February 1994. Under new manager Sandy Clark, Hearts avoided relegation with a spirited late rally.

Dave McPherson scores in Hearts' 4-2 victory over Rangers in the Scottish Cup in February 1995. The team, now under the control of Tommy McLean, progressed to the Semi-finals, but then lost to Airdrie. Another relegation battle was won in the 1994/95 season.

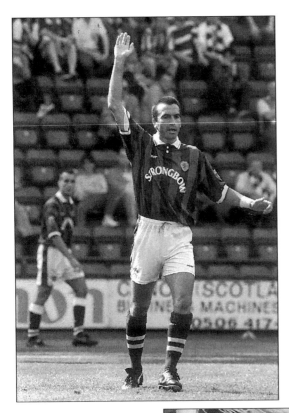

Pasquale Bruno, one of the shrewd signings made by Jim Jefferies after he took over as Hearts manager in July 1995. Jim's astute moves in the transfer market and encouragement of young players raised the spirit at Tynecastle and the team finished a much improved fourth in the League. Hearts also reached the 1996 Scottish Cup Final, but Rangers proved too strong and defeated the 'Maroons' 5-1.

David Weir scores against Kilmarnock in August 1996. The international defender scored in the League Cup Final as well, where Hearts lost 4-3 to Rangers after a thrilling contest. Once again, the team finished fourth in the League.

How Hearts' Scottish Cup heroes lined up in the final against Rangers on Saturday 16 May 1998.

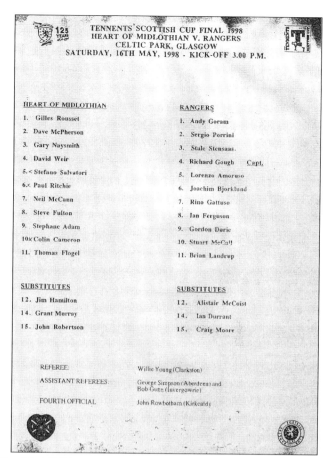

TENNENTS' SCOTTISH CUP FINAL 1998
HEART OF MIDLOTHIAN V. RANGERS
CELTIC PARK, GLASGOW
SATURDAY, 16TH MAY, 1998 - KICK-OFF 3.00 P.M.

HEART OF MIDLOTHIAN

1. Gilles Rousset
2. Dave McPherson
3. Gary Naysmith
4. David Weir
5. Stefano Salvatori
6. Paul Ritchie
7. Neil McCann
8. Steve Fulton
9. Stephane Adam
10. Colin Cameron
11. Thomas Flogel

RANGERS

1. Andy Goram
2. Sergio Porrini
3. Stale Stensaas.
4. Richard Gough   Capt.
5. Lorenzo Amoruso
6. Joachim Bjorklund
7. Rino Gattuso
8. Ian Ferguson
9. Gordon Durie
10. Stuart McCall
11. Brian Laudrup

SUBSTITUTES

12. Jim Hamilton
14. Grant Murray
15. John Robertson

SUBSTITUTES

12. Alistair McCoist
14. Ian Durrant
15. Craig Moore

REFEREE: Willie Young (Clarkston)

ASSISTANT REFEREES: George Simpson (Aberdeen) and
                      Bob Gunn (Invergowrie)

FOURTH OFFICIAL   John Rowbotham (Kirkcaldy)

Colin Cameron opens the scoring from the penalty spot in the 1998 Scottish Cup Final.

Hearts' Scottish Cup-winning heroes enjoy a day of celebration at Tynecastle in May 1998. Goals by Colin Cameron and Stephane Adam brought the Cup back to Edinburgh for the first time since 1956. After an excellent season, Hearts also finished third in the League.

Printed in Great Britain
by Amazon

41235505R00075